The Nature In Your Soul

Ashley Menssa

The Nature In Your Soul
Copyright © 2020 by Ashley Menssa

All rights reserved. No part of this publication may be reproduced, distributed, or transmitted in any form or by any means, including photocopying, recording, or other electronic or mechanical methods, without the prior written permission of the author, except in the case of brief quotations embodied in critical reviews and certain other non-commercial uses permitted by copyright law.

Tellwell Talent
www.tellwell.ca

ISBN
978-0-2288-2231-8 (Paperback)
978-0-2288-2232-5 (eBook)

To those who have built and broken me;
This is for you.

The Sun

The day our world
Lives in peace
Is the day
The sun
Will smile upon our souls,
And flowers
Will bloom
In our hearts,
Among abundant
Fields of
Joy.

When I picture my future,
My happiness is not found
In a man.
It is found in a cup of lemon tea,
On a rainy Sunday morning,
And the early traffic
Of London streets.

That night,
The stars took me
Into their arms,
With bright eyes
And warm smiles,
And said,
"Welcome home."

The smell of guitar strings
Is the sight
Of an old poet's soul
Standing in the mirror,
Holding a glass of whiskey,
And breathing in the sweet distraction
Of a midnight cigarette.

Chocolate and strawberries
Feel like
Fireplaces and fuzzy socks,
A lover's fingers
Tangled in your own,
And they whisper
Ever so softly,
Everything your dreams are made of,
In your ear.

People are shallow waters,
That are waded in
To relieve those of the need to swim,
But there are some people
Whose waters lack no depth,
And only in their knowledge and creativity,
Would I wish to drown.

I need more nights
Filled with the blissful
Hovering between sleep
And ecstasy.

Madness is security
And comfort in chaos,
Peace is contentment and
Happiness in serenity.
Nothing have I learned
In this life,
Except, that I am
Wildly,
Beautifully,
Mad.

Your voice
Is the supple undertone
Of the burning clouds;
When the sun is dying,
And the cerulean sky
Is still awake.

Your smile
Is etched in my thoughts,
Mine?
Well, it hasn't disappeared since.

Nothing should we
Fear more,
Than the innate simplicity
Of being
Only alive.

I am like the sun,
Captured
In a raindrop.
Small, but powerful,
Common,
But upon deeper consideration,
Unprecedented.

My fingertips are tingling
With the touch of you,
Your whispered words
Are ringing ever so softly,
In this empty void.
Soft hands
Tangled in my hair,
The taste of you, imprinted,
On my favourite, black sweater.
And baby, my love
I'm going to drink you in,
And hold you close.
I am addicted.

When your skin is on mine,
It ignites a fire in my soul,
Making my heart
Burn…
For you.

Your smile
Nurtures
The blooming flowers
Of my soul.
Bringing them life,
Every time you laugh.

I hope you become so happy,
That you dance
And sing,
To every song you hear.
I hope you become so happy,
That you smile
At every stranger you pass.
I hope, that you,
Beautiful you,
Are happy.

There are so many beautiful people,
In love with so many beautiful things,
For this world,
To be filled with so much
Hate.

My darling,
Once you love
Every ounce of yourself;
Every scar,
Every freckle,
Every curl,
Every smile,
Every fleck of colour in your eyes,
Every struggling breath,
And the crooked tooth next to the curve of your lips,
Then,
You will be happy.

He was a summer boy.
With sandy hair, and grassy eyes,
Sun-kissed skin, and a late-night-drive kind of smile,
Oh, I fell in love,
With a summer boy.

From the moment
I saw those
Blue eyes;
I knew,
That I had no choice
But,
To fall in love.

You make me forget
What the sadness
Felt like.

Gaze at the stars with me,
Let's fall in love,
With everything that I see in your eyes.

You are a constellation,
In a sky
Of scattered lights.

Marked on your skin
Is every hardship,
That you survived
Every aching memory,
Marked on your skin,
Is strength.

Your arms are my safe haven.
My serenity amidst
The chaos

When you lose focus,
It becomes more beautiful.

The most beautiful words
That I have written,
Were of you,
And our safely kept memories
Folded
Underneath my pillow.

The pain I felt yesterday,
Has made me grow today,
And I will heal tomorrow.

The evergreen in your smile
And the sun in your hazel eyes
Makes me hope,
That in a field of sunflowers,
You'll pick a lilac.

For the sake
Of feeling,
Do.

I am
The sun,
And,
I am
The rain.
It is
The nature
In my soul
That makes me
A paradox.

The Rain

Sometimes I forget
That we never really said,
Goodbye.
It was just a "see you later."
I had looked at you,
Hoping to see those eyes again.
Those beautiful, brown eyes
That undressed my mind,
But you just stared ahead.
I turned,
And walked out of the door.
Maybe that was my goodbye,
That final look at you.
It was good enough in the end,
But I suppose,
It would have been nice
To know that our last kiss
Was really
Our last.

I feel something
Nostalgic
When I touch your lips.

My fingers smell like filters,
But I haven't smoked in days
And I'm talking to you
And... I feel whole
As I look
At my shattered pieces,
Scattered at my feet.

My fingers are stained,
With the attempt
Of trying to erase you.
Once the paint is gone,
I'll clean my brushes
And my hands.
I'll hang the memories of you,
Of us,
Up on the wall
You used to push me up against.
People will walk by,
They'll say how nice it is.
I'll just smile, and nod my head
Because they have no idea,
How lovely
It really was.

I feel like
I can't get over you,
Because we took
Our broken pieces,
And rebuilt ourselves
With
Each other.

I'm sorry
That I fell so deeply for you.
I am sorry,
I loved you more than myself.
I am sorry,
For that 5 a.m. drunk call.
You believed every lie that I slurred.
I am sorry,
That I wanted you to hurt, as much as I did.
I am sorry,
That I wanted you to miss me too.
I'm sorry.

You said,
That you were addicted;
But there was no rehab,
After you quit me.
Baby, my love,
It was just
A new bottle
Of pills.

Make love to my soul,
Undress my heart,
Speak to my eyes…
And
Stay

Maybe we were meant to be,
But we had one too many
Drunken calls,
And 3 a.m. texts,
To call it love.
So now,
With my lips on yours,
And your hands on my hips,
We're just friends.

Either stay,
Or leave.
No one pleasures
In the angst
Of your façade.

I've already caught my breath.
So stop trying
To push me back
Under the water.

We have seen
Too much
Of this broken world,
To be considered innocent.

I both fear
And adore
Being alone.
Simply because
My mind
Has both the power
To warm,
And chill,
My soul.

I feel
Powerful
In your absence.
Once again, I am in control
Of my own chaos

I had no tears left,
That day,
The sky cried for me.

I have found
That so many things,
In this fucking world,
Are far more beautiful,
At a distance.

I deal with my pain by pretending I don't feel it.
Eventually,
Oh, eventually,
I'll fool myself too.

I was scared when I fell in love.
It was all too good,
And I couldn't believe it.
I had become so addicted to the chaos
And being with you,
Had calmed the storm inside of me.
You cleared my skies.
But baby, just know,
I am better a hurricane,
Than a rainbow.

Never have I been one
To speak about the turbulent waters
Of my soul.
But when I choose to write,
The pages become soaked.

Walking on the street are people,
Drowning their souls,
In a neon cathedral.
In an attempt, so feeble,
To find some freedom, maybe a rush;
That is now, almost always,
Illegal.

I want to wash away
Every bad memory,
Every painful wound.
I want to erase
Your charcoal drawing of pain
And paint your bright soul
With watercolours.

Everything
That was once ours,
Is tainted,
With the stained memory
Of our once
Beautiful love.

Come,
Hold me.
Hold my empty
Soul.
Hold my tattered
Heart.
Come,
Lover,
And hold me.

Follow me
Into the dark
Abyss of my
Empty heart.
And follow me,
Into the turbulent waters
Of my soul;
And we will sink to the bottom,
Of what we once
Called love.

I am searching,
To find one,
At least one,
Beautiful reason
To live.

I am feeling
All too much,
And all too little,
To be sane.

I am on the
Self-destructive path
Of forgetting you.

You left me
Breathless,
Helpless,
And in love
All at once.

We had
So much more time
To fall
Deeper into
Each other.

www.ingramcontent.com/pod-product-compliance
Lightning Source LLC
LaVergne TN
LVHW072023060526
838200LV00058B/4652